BE STILL
and talk with
GOD DAILY

SANDRA RICHARDSON
FOREWORD BY: YAKINEA MARIE

Be Still and Talk With God Daily
Copyright © 2022 Sandra Richardson

All rights reserved. No part of this book may be reproduced or transmitted in any form or any means, electronic or mechanical; including photocopy, recording, or any information storage and retrieval system for any reason without the express written permission of the author.

Published by SRych Publishing, an imprint of The Rych Collective, LLC
F.A.I.T.H. - Facing All Indecisions Through Him is a trademark of Sandra Richardson

Exterior Art by Rych Productions, Tevyn Richardson-Owner

Acknowledgement: Wyvern Wallace, Editor

Scripture quotations marked (NLT), are taken from the New Living Translation, copyright © 1996, 2004, 2015 by Tyndale House Foundation. Used by permission of Tyndale House Publishers, a division of Tyndale House Ministries, Carol Stream, Illinois 60188. All rights reserved.

Scripture quotations marked (AMP) are taken from the Amplified ® Bible, copyright © 2015 by the Lockman Foundation. Used by permission, (www.Lockman.org).

Scripture quotations marked (NIV) are taken from the Holy Bible, New International Version ®, NIV ®. Copyright © 1973, 1978, 1984, 2011 by Biblica, Inc.™ Used by permission of Zondervan. All rights reserved worldwide. (www.zondervan.com). The NIV and New International Version are trademarks registered in the United States Patent and Trademark Office by Biblica Inc. ™

Scripture quotations marked (NKJV) are taken from the New King James Version ®. Copyright © 1982 by Thomas Nelson. Used by permission. All rights reserved.

Scripture quotations marked (TPT) are taken from the Passion Translation ®. Copyright © 2017, 2018, 2020 by Passion & Fire Ministries, Inc. Used by permission. All rights reserved. ThePassionTranslation.com.

Scripture quotations marked (GNT) are taken from the Good News Bible © 1994 published by the Bible Societies/HarperCollins Publishers Ltd UK, Good News Bible © American Bible Society 1966, 1971, 1976, 1992. Used with permission.

Scripture quotations marked (MSG) are taken from the Message. Copyright © 1993, 1994, 1995, 1996, 2000, 2001, 2002. Used by permission of NavPress Publishing Group. http://www.navpress.com.

Scripture quotations marked (MEV) are from the Modern English Version. Copyright © 2014 by Military Bible Association. Used by permission. All rights reserved.

ISBN: 979-8-9863816-0-2

BE STILL
&
Talk With God Daily

This is the beginning of a new day and

you have been given this day to use as you will.

You can waste it or use it for good.

What you do today is important because

you are exchanging a day of your life for it.

When tomorrow comes, this day will be gone forever.

In its place is something that you have left behind...

Let it be something good.

–Author Unknown–

CONTENTS

Foreword 4
Introduction 5

Day 1	Just Breathe 6
Day 2	God's Plan 8
Day 3	Rest Margins 10
Day 4	Time 12
Day 5	Waiting 14
Day 6	Patience 16
Day 7	Priorities 18
Day 8	Prayer 20
Day 9	Procrastination 22
Day 10	Focus 24
Day 11	Self-Discipline 26
Day 12	Distractions 28
Day 13	Commitment 30
Day 14	Consistency 32
Day 15	Obedience 34
Day 16	Wisdom 36
Day 17	Balance 38
Day 18	Who Am I? 40
Day 19	I Am Enough 42
Day 20	El Hayyay 44
Day 21	My Source 46
Day 22	Faith 48
Day 23	Victory 50
Day 24	Accountability 52
Day 25	Clutter/Declutter 54
Day 26	Elohe Chaseddi 56
Day 27	Forgive 58
Day 28	Gratitude 60
Day 29	Favor 62
Day 30	Integrity 64

About the Author 66

FOREWORD

How priceless it is to sit in the presence of God, knowing that He hears every word you speak. What an honor it is to be so loved by God that He would take out the time to answer you. Jeremiah 33:3 reminds us of this truth. God wants to talk with you.

A conversation with God is not to be taken lightly. Why? Because you have the opportunity to dialogue with the Supreme Sovereign God. Yes, dialogue. Many make the error of approaching God expecting a one-sided talk, but when you come to a place of stillness, understand that your conversation with God is not a monologue but a dialogue. A dialogue is between two or more individuals regarding a shared subject that has the power to inspire, enlighten and ignite the listener.

When talking with God, in order to receive what is released one must master the position of first being still. I'm reminded of the scripture in Psalms 46:10 where the Lord says, "Be still and know that I am God...". It's in the stillness that we are able to truly hear God. It's in the stillness that we are able to truly talk with God undistracted.

In Sandra's devotional "Be Still and Talk With God Daily", you will go on a journey of understanding the power of being in God's presence. You will be guided daily and inspired to build a lasting relationship in the presence of God consistently. There is rest in being still. There is power in talking with God.

Yakinea Marie
Founder of SheCEO Global

INTRODUCTION

In the hustle and bustle of our daily lives, we get so busy as a human doing that we forget to be a human being. We are constantly doing something. It seems that the world thinks that the busier the better. The dictionary defines busy as engaged in action; occupied. My definition of busy is:

> **B**owing down
> **U**nder
> **S**ociety's
> **Y**oke

What are the things that society has us bound by that keeps us sooo busy? Is it surfing the internet, watching reality shows, scrolling on social media, playing video games, watching Netflix, watching movies or sitcoms, sleeping, gambling, shopping, hanging with friends, or going to the club?

Sometimes we are so busy that we think we don't even have time to talk to God before we start our day. Let me just tell you, if we are too busy for God, we definitely need to take a step back and prioritize our calendars!

We need to slow down and allow God the opportunity to refresh us through His Word and through spending time with Him. This devotional will provide a daily reading to help us focus on spending time with God. It will be a time to get into God's presence, reflect on His goodness, all that He has done and continues to do for us on a daily basis. It will allow us to take a moment to breathe and listen to what God wants to speak into our lives.

> **'Just a little talk with Jesus makes it right'**

JUST BREATHE

Be still and know that I am God. I will be exalted among the nations, I will be exalted in the earth.

Psalm 46:10 (NIV)

*H*ave you ever seen anyone make a gesture to take a deep breath and say woosah? The definition of woosah is a state of clarity and calmness. Psalm 46:10 tells us to take a deep breath in and release. You are to stop striving and let go of your concerns. Some will say you are not worried and everything is under control, but is it really? Just calm down, recognize and understand God in His sovereignty. God already has it figured out.

God is exalted among the nations and in all the earth. How about sitting still and allowing Him to be exalted in your life? He is ready to handle the situation for you, if you let him.

'Let It Go!'

GOD'S PLAN

And by the seventh day God completed His work which He had done, and He rested (ceased) on the seventh day from all His work which He had done.

Genesis 2:2 (AMP)

When God created the heavens and the earth, He wrote out His plan because He knew He had a lot to accomplish. Let's look at an overview of each day.

    Day 1 - Light
    Day 2 - Atmosphere/Firmament
    Day 3 - Dry ground & plants
    Day 4 - Sun, moon and stars
    Day 5 - Birds & sea creatures
    Day 6 - Land animals & humans
    Day 7 - The sabbath of rest

As we look at day 7, God didn't haphazardly decide to rest because He was tired. It was part of His initial plan. He already knew that if He didn't put the principle of rest into motion, we would not see it as a priority. God knew that we would be on a continuous treadmill, trying to live our best life through our own self sufficiency. God wants us to thrive and live our best lives to the fullest, but without compromising our rest.

'Take a Load Off'

REST MARGINS

As we enter into God's faith-rest life we cease from our own works, just as God celebrates his finished works and rests in them.

Hebrews 4:10 (TPT)

As Christians, it should be our goal to be like Christ. Today's scripture reminds us that God rested. If God rested, doesn't that mean we should also rest? Do you feel guilty if you set aside time to rest?

Margin is a boundary; the rest that is purposefully built into our daily schedule. It is the space between rest and exhaustion. If we get to the point where our physical body is ready to collapse from a lack of rest, we have crossed over into the margins. We have ventured into the space between our load and our limit. When we get here, we must realize that we have entered the zone where enough is enough!

We should have boundaries set on purpose that will stop us before we get to that point. We have to learn to say NO and not feel guilty about it. If our bodies are telling us to rest, we must listen. Follow in the footsteps of the Maker and rest! It may mean actually scheduling rest as an appointment on the calendar. We must make that appointment with ourselves equally as important as an appointment with someone else. We are our own greatest asset and totally worth it!

'Commit To Rest'

Day 4

TIME

So, then, be careful how you live. Do not be unwise but wise, making the best use of your time because the times are evil. Therefore, do not be foolish, but understand what the Lord's will is.

Ephesians 5:15-17 (MEV)

Time is such a small word, but has such a large impact on our lives. So often we hear or even say, I didn't have enough time, I ran out of time, I needed more time, I need more hours in the day, time flies and/or time waits for no one.

As Christians, as we are managing our time, we must make sure to seek God in everything we do. We should organize our time and plan wisely for the future, always seeking to do this within God's will for our lives. As we continue to meditate on scripture, God will direct our lives. We must be sure to listen to the wisdom of God as He directs and guides us to keep us from wasting time.

Let's look at the word time from a different perspective:

> **T**rust in God's Word
> **I**nvite God into your circumstances
> **M**eet God daily
> **E**stablish boundaries

When we trust in the Word of God, we are already on the right path to wise time management. Once we invite God into our circumstances, we will avoid making the wrong decisions and heading in the wrong direction. Meeting with God every day is one of the daily essential vitamins necessary for a vibrant life! Establishing boundaries is so very important because there will be people and other distractions that come along, but we have to learn to say NO!

'T.I.M.E.'

WAITING

Here's what I've learned through it all: Don't give up; don't be impatient; be entwined as one with the Lord. Be brave and courageous and never lose hope. Yes, keep on waiting for He will never disappoint you!

Psalms 27:14 (TPT)

The definition of wait is to stay where one is or delay action until a particular time or until something else happens. The bible defines waiting as being aware through all the senses of what is occurring around you and discerning the right time to do the next thing. Waiting is pretty significant in that it appears 154 times in the King James version of the Bible.

How did you react the last time you had to wait in line? Did you immediately get an attitude? Did your face scrunch up and your whole demeanor change? Maybe you kept looking at your watch. When it was your time to be serviced, were you rude because you were tired of waiting? On the other hand, did you choose to keep a pleasant look on your face and wait patiently? Did you take the opportunity to just relax for a few minutes? Were you pleasant and thankful when it was your time to be serviced? Internally, the results of being rude and unpleasant to others are frustration, annoyance and even anger.

In the grand scheme of things, how you wait is so very important. When you're waiting on God, you should really rest in God. When you rest in God, you are confident that He will make things happen when they are supposed to happen. You don't have to put a time limit on God because He will always be right on time. He will answer with your best interests in mind. Through the process of resting in God, you get renewed strength and become stronger! As you rest, remember that God's love is unfailing, His provision is faithful, His resources are unlimited and He absolutely cares for you!

'Rest in God'

PATIENCE

Quiet your heart in His presence and wait patiently for Yahweh. And don't think for a moment that the wicked, in their prosperity, are better off than you.

Psalms 37:7 (TPT)

*P*atience is commonly defined as the capacity to accept or tolerate delay, trouble or suffering without getting angry or upset. Patience is also a virtue from God and is one of the fruits of the Spirit. So many of us lack patience. Today's society wants everything right now today or maybe even yesterday. When we are driving, the other car is always going too slow and we have to pass them. In the grocery store, the lines are too long and we go from one line to the next because we don't want to wait. At the restaurant, the server gets backlash because the kitchen is taking too long to prepare the food. When we are impatient, we become anxious. Philippians 4:6 reminds us that we are to be anxious for nothing.

The enemy wants you to miss out on what God has for you by giving you the impression you are missing out on something if you don't move right now! He wants you to think you are losing out if you wait to see what God has to say. The Passion Translation of Psalm 46:10a states to surrender your anxiety. Be still and realize that I am God! The next time you are inclined to complain, remember to just be still. God will provide supernatural insight into the situation. Impatience shows that we don't trust God. If we are guilty of being impatient, it is time to make the necessary adjustments in order for us to patiently walk in the plan that God has predestined for our lives.

'Slow Your Roll'

PRIORITIES

The Lord answered her, "Martha, my beloved Martha. Why are you upset and troubled, pulled away by all these many distractions? Mary has discovered the one thing most important by choosing to sit at my feet. She is undistracted, and I won't take this privilege from her."

Luke 10:41-42 (TPT)

*P*riority is a concern, interest or desire that comes before all others. A priority needs to be dealt with first. It is the right to take precedence and precede others in order, rank and privilege.

How many times have we started on the right path, but somewhere along the way our priorities got a little bit twisted? Okay, more than just a little bit! I have certainly had some Martha, Martha moments in my life. Jesus was very courteous to Martha when she asked him to make Mary get up and help her. In today's society, Jesus would say Martha, you are worried about the wrong thing! Your priorities are all **Out Of Order!** Your sister, Mary knows what time it is and she has her priorities together. You need to go sit down over there by Mary so you can learn something. Those chicken wings will be there when I finish teaching!

On a serious note, how many of us need to stop striving in the world and starting thriving in the Word? According to Matthew 6:33, when we seek God first, everything else will follow. We need to look at all those good things we are doing and line them up in order behind the God things God told us to do. Sandra, Sandra, … girl make sure you get your priorities straight, so God will not have to pull your coat tail and sit you down!

'First Things First'

PRAYER

Don't be pulled in different directions or worried about a thing. Be saturated in prayer throughout each day, offering your faith-filled requests before God with overflowing gratitude. Tell Him every detail of your life.

Philippians 4:6 (TPT)

Prayer is simply having a conversation with God. It is a direct line of communication with the one who made us, the platform and firm foundation needed to build our lives in and through Christ.

As we pray to God daily, we must learn to be still in His presence and give Him the opportunity to speak. Have you ever been in a conversation with someone and they just kept talking and talking and talking, not giving you a chance to speak? As the old saying goes, you couldn't get a word in edgewise! That's how God feels when we do all the talking and He can't get a word in edgewise. Let's make a conscious effort to not monopolize the conversation.

Prayer should be scheduled as well as spontaneous throughout the day. It is a good idea to start your morning with prayer. Psalms 5:3, says "In the morning, O Lord, You will hear my voice; In the morning I will prepare a prayer and a sacrifice for You and watch and wait for You to speak to my heart." (AMP)

As we take the time to pray, we must remember that nothing is too small or too large to pray about. There is nothing to be embarrassed about with our Father God. There is absolutely nothing too hard for God to handle. God is concerned about what concerns us. Let's work on building a more intimate relationship with God as we spend more intentional time with Him through prayer.

'Talk With God'

PROCRASTINATION

Slackers will know what it means to be poor, while the hard worker becomes wealthy.

Proverbs 10:4 (TPT)

*P*rocrastination means to defer action. It is to delay doing something until a later time or until the last minute because you do not want to do it. This even applies to hitting the snooze button to delay getting out of bed until the last minute because you don't want to get up. Do not start your day by procrastinating. Get your BLESSED self up to experience this new day that the Lord has made!

Procrastination usually happens when people fear, dread or have anxiety about an important task. This leads to just handling low priority tasks or not doing anything at all. Procrastination generally occurs because of an inability to self-regulate behavior. This lack of sufficient self control leads to someone acting against their better judgment, even when he/she realizes that doing so could have a negative outcome.

I have had many instances in my life where I have procrastinated and procrastinated and procrastinated! This devotional you are reading right now was developed under a cloud of procrastination. I had to persevere and keep pushing until it was finished. As you take an assessment of life's decisions, identify any areas that were clouded by procrastination. Make a conscious effort to not let them hinder you in the future. Do not be like the slacker mentioned above in Proverbs 10. Make sure you are the one who becomes wealthy! Don't have an arrogant disregard for God's instructions. Do not assume that He owes you another opportunity tomorrow to do what you could have done today!

'What are you Waiting for?'

FOCUS

Don't allow yourself to be sidetracked for even a moment or take a detour that leads to darkness.

Proverbs 4:27 (TPT)

How many of you have ever been driving and hit a pothole? I'm sure a lot of you saw the pothole up ahead and made a quick decision to avoid the pothole. Then a few seconds later, bop! You hit the pothole! The reason why you hit the pothole was because your focus was off. Instead of focusing on the path around the pothole, you were focusing on the pothole.

Focus is defined as the concentration of attention or energy on something in particular; to give your full attention to what you are doing or to what is happening.

If you have ever made goals you didn't keep or a New Year's resolution that did not make it past January, it was probably because of a lack of focus. A lack of focus is the number one reason why people do not reach their goals and maximize their potential. If you focus on what you want, you will get it. If you focus on what you don't want, you will get that as well. Focus will determine your future. What is God calling you to do in the future?

As you look at all of the good ideas you have, you must first determine which idea is the God idea that needs to take priority. Set your heart and mind to press toward the mark and get it done! Your focus will determine your future. Let it shine bright like a diamond!

F.O.C.U.S.
Follow One Course Until Successful!

SELF-DISCIPLINE

A person without self-control is like a house with its doors and windows knocked out.

Proverbs 25:28 (MSG)

*S*elf discipline is the ability to pursue what one thinks is right despite temptations to abandon it. The Oxford dictionary defines self-discipline as the ability to make yourself do something. For some of you, it took a whole lot of discipline to pick up this devotional this morning! Look at you, you did it!

How important is self-discipline? Yesterday, we talked about focus. Today we will learn that self-discipline allows you to stay focused on your goals by enabling you to stay in control of yourself and your reactions. Discipline will empower you to go beyond the ordinary and reach the extraordinary.

Self-discipline is the bridge that you will walk across to reach your accomplishments. The more you practice it, just like going to the gym, the stronger you will become. It may be painful while you are going through, but just think about the big payoff! Those "discipline" muscles look good on you!

The late Myles Munroe stated "when people pay to see you they are paying for your discipline." What the world sees is a direct result of all the discipline and hard work done behind the scenes.

'I See You!'

DISTRACTIONS

Yes, feast on all the treasures of the heavenly realm and fill your thoughts with heavenly realities, and not with the distractions of the natural realm.

Colossians 3:2 (TPT)

Distractions, distractions, distractions...so many distractions. Distraction means to draw apart or pull in a different direction. I should have counted the number of times I was distracted as I was writing this devotional. It seems like there was always some type of distraction to deter me from accomplishing my goal. Distractions eat away at our time and attention like parasites. Before you realize it, two or three hours have passed! Distractions shift our attention from something of greater importance to something of lesser importance. The enemy may deceive us into thinking that a particular matter is urgent and needs to be handled immediately. It might just be that the matter is truly important and needs to be handled, but it's not so urgent that it cannot wait until you finish the task at hand. It can wait!

Distractions come in many forms. One that is probably familiar to most people is social media. The intention of making one simple happy birthday post can turn into hours of scrolling! Close family members and friends can be a distraction. They may call just for a health check, but end up talking for 30 minutes telling you about what happened to cousin Susie. Identify what your distractions are and make a decision to not be controlled by them.

When it comes to spending time with God, if you need to get up earlier to have your devotional time without interference or distractions, go ahead and set your alarm clock for an earlier time. God wants us to spend time with Him. Thank Him for grace to be able to spend that quality time with Him on a daily basis.

'We Can Do This'

COMMITMENT

Commit your actions to the Lord, and your plans will succeed.

Proverbs 16:3 (NLT)

*I*n the Hebrew language the word commit means to roll. Think of rolling something to the Lord. The idea is completely giving something over to God while depending on Him. We are offering everything we do completely to the Lord when we commit our works to him.

How many of you have been playing ball with a toddler and you rolled the ball to them and they rolled it back to you? Envision yourself rolling your ball of cares and challenges to God. He is not going to roll it back because you rolled it to Him for resolution. Since God didn't answer in your timeframe, you decided you could handle it on your own. So what did you do? You just sashayed on over and picked the ball back up! When you commit something to God, you should trust Him enough to handle the situation. The scripture clearly states our plans will succeed when we commit them to the Lord. When you don't stay committed, sometimes outcomes are not favorable. Afterwards, you may get selective amnesia as you wonder why things didn't work the way YOU planned. Selah...Pause and think about that!

Sacrifice, purpose, patience and determination are key factors in maintaining commitment. In order to go to another level in life, we have to go to another level in God. We have an advantage when we get into divine alignment with God's assignment and stay committed.

'Do not be Double-Minded'

CONSISTENCY

So let's not allow ourselves to get fatigued from doing good. At the right time we will harvest a good crop if we don't give up, or quit.

Galatians 6:9 (MSG)

Invision a football field. There is a goal post at each end and the 50 yard line is right in the middle. Your goals represent one goal post and your achievements represent the other goal post. Your consistency is right in the middle at the 50 yard line. Consistency is the key to successfully advancing your goals down the field to score a touchdown with your achievements.

While on the field, you may get tackled a few times, but don't stay down. Call on the Holy Spirit to play defense and block for you. The Holy Spirit is aware of dangers seen and unseen and knows just where to position Himself to block the next play that Satan has set up. You will also have to play offense and get in the Word so you will be ready to put God's Word on any situation that comes up and be able to keep from fumbling the ball. Don't be afraid to ask the Ref for a time-out. You have to take time to pray and get the game plan from Coach Jesus. You have to be familiar with the play book. You must also listen to the Coach on how to execute the plays and consistently follow the plays the way they were designed. Consistency will lead to the breakthrough you need to carry that punt return all the way to achievement!

'Touchdown!'

OBEDIENCE

"Yes," said Jesus, "but God will bless all who listen to the Word of God and carefully obey everything they hear."

Luke 11:28 (TPT)

Biblical obedience to God means to hear, trust, submit and surrender to God and His Word. The bible dictionary defines it as to hear God's Word and act accordingly. Obedience to God is a way to worship Him as well as a way to get closer to Him by showing our love for Him.

As our scripture reflects, we are rewarded when we first listen, then obey God's Word. It is so frustrating when you are talking to someone and you know they hear you, but they are really not listening. Sometimes I will make the comment that I guess I must have been just talking to myself. I wonder if that's how God feels when He gives us instructions to do something and we either were not listening or have made a decision to not obey.

So many times we ask God to speak to us, only to decide that what He said is not what we wanted to hear. We start asking, was that really God or was that the devil? Did He mean for me to do that now or can I wait a few months? We have to be able to trust God enough to obey Him even when we don't understand. The true measure of hearing from God is our action/reaction after hearing what He said.

'Obedience is Better Than Sacrifice'

Day 16

WISDOM

And if anyone longs to be wise, ask God for wisdom and He will give it! He won't see your lack of wisdom as an opportunity to scold you over your failures, but He will overwhelm your failures with His generous grace.

James 1:5 (TPT)

Wisdom is defined as the ability to use your knowledge, experience and careful judgment to make good decisions. Godly wisdom starts with fearing God and shutting out the enemy's schemes, which results in a holy life that enables us to prepare ourselves for eternity. When we operate in Godly wisdom, we strive to see things from God's perspective and exemplify biblical values. Walking in Godly wisdom will cause us to make decisions that are different from our natural inclination. Wisdom empowers us to rise above situations and reign above our circumstances.

James 1:5 tells to ask for wisdom and He is delighted to give it. However, God wants you to ask in unwavering faith and not doubt. We must constantly pursue wisdom. The book of Proverbs is an excellent source for studying wisdom and practicing what you learn. Your life should be able to advertise the wisdom of God and bring glory to Him. If you want to build up your wisdom muscles, try reading one Proverb each day. This daily dose of wisdom will be exhibited in the applied knowledge of the ways of God.

'The Principal Thing'

Day 17

BALANCE

So above all, constantly seek God's kingdom and His righteousness, then all these less important things will be given to you abundantly.

Matthew 6:33 (TPT)

Balance comes when we put our entire lives into God's hands as we seek first the Kingdom of God. If we work as unto the Lord and live our lives to please Him, our lives will naturally line up with God's perfect will. As we continue to pursue the heart of God and to be led by His Spirit, we will find constant renewal and refreshment. If we are first and foremost honoring God with our every thought and deed, then His peace, joy and rest will be manifested. God wants us to rest in HIm as we find balance in our lives.

Balance starts within and is developed internally rather than externally. Balance is being in the moment of what we are involved in at that particular time, being careful to not be pulled in multiple directions. There can be chaos all around and we can pull inner peace and strength from within and not let the environment get us off sync. When we are balanced, we are in a state of mental and emotional rest. We must realize that balance will not look the same for everyone. What constitutes balance for a single mother of three young children is much different than what balance looks like for a married Mom of three, who is now an empty nester. We cannot fall into the trap of looking at someone else's life and comparing ours to theirs. We must look to God and make His will a priority in our lives. If He is first, all other things in life will balance out!

'Seek God'

Day 18

WHO AM I?

And have made us kings and priests to our God; and we shall reign on the earth.

Revelations 5:10 (NKJV)

When you know your true identity, you don't have to be told by others who you are. As the scripture in Revelations 5 tells us, we are kings and priests. God created us for an eternal relationship with Him as a part of His royal family. As a part of this family, we have dominion on the earth. This means to govern, rule or have power over the kingdom, which is the king's domain.

As you answer the question of who you are, make sure you view yourself as God sees you. You should not attempt to live up to anyone's expectations other than God's. So many people walk around with an inferiority complex as a result of comparing themselves to other people. Take your power back as you walk in your own potential. No one can make you feel inferior without your consent. From this day forward, veto that consent!

Knowing your God given identity gives you validation and increases your faith. You know that you're already equipped to do what God is calling you to do and you have faith that He will do the work through you. Matthew 5:48 tells us to grow up, live like the kingdom subjects we are and live out our God-created identity.

'Claim Your Identity'

Day 19

I AM ENOUGH

But you are a chosen people, a royal priesthood, a holy nation, God's special possession.

I Peter 2:9a (NIV)

The scripture in I Peter 2:9 let's us know first of all that God chose you. When He chose you, He was choosing a possession that is greater and different from what is usual. You are a special possession. Therefore, you don't ever have to wonder if you are enough. You are covered by the blood of Jesus who makes you righteous and enough for whatever comes your way.

Even though there may be times when you think you are not enough, the scripture in John 8:32 (NLT) states "And you will know the truth, and the truth will set you free." You must walk in the truth that you are enough just like you are. When it appears that others are prospering ahead of you, do not feel inadequate or less than. God has a plan for your life in spite of what appears to be happening at the current state. Just because it looks like you are losing, does not mean that you are!

Knowing that you are enough, means that you are pretty enough, smart enough, athletic enough, funny enough, lovable enough, skilled enough and worthy enough. Renew your mind to the truth of God's Word which says you are able to accomplish all things through Christ Jesus. God's Word does not have to be validated by man. **You are enough with nothing else attached.**

'You've Got This'

Day 20

EL HAYYAY
THE GOD OF MY LIFE

And this Light never fails to shine through darkness-Light that darkness could not overcome!

John 1:5 (TPT)

*I*f you have ever walked from total darkness into a bright light, you really had to focus in order to see. Your eyes were so accustomed to the darkness, the light somewhat blinded you for a moment. You probably put your hands up to your forehead to form a shield over your eyes.

When you walk this journey called life without God, it's like making your way through life in total darkness. You start reaching out trying to grasp whatever you can get your hands on, desperate to make it to a place where something is familiar. During this process, you get impatient and make poor decisions while you stumble through day to day circumstances. You feel like you have lost all sense of direction.

This is the time to turn to the light that God provides. This is done by studying His Word and seeking His presence through prayer. You must listen to discern His voice and be obedient. He may want to lead you in a new direction and place your feet on a different path. God is not surprised by anything that happens in your life because He is the God of your life. When you are ready to seek His way, He is ready to bring you into the light.

'Let the Light Shine'

Day 21

MY SOURCE

I am the sprouting vine and you're my branches. As you live in union with me as your source, fruitfulness will stream from within you.

John 15:5a (TPT)

The vine is the source and sustenance of life for the branches. The source is someone or something that provides what is wanted or needed. The roots of the vine serve to anchor the plant to the soil. Jesus is our vine and as branches, we look to Him as our source to provide what we need to live a life that honors and glorifies Him. He pumps life into us as we remain anchored in Him to provide guidance and direction in our daily lives.

If we live a Christlike life, obeying Him and following His commands, we will bear fruit that others may see His good works through us. Ephesians 2:10b(TPT) tells us that even before we were born, God planned our destiny and the good works we would do to fulfill it! As we remain and abide in Jesus, we are able to carry out those good works that are already predestined for us to do.

'Remain'

Day 22

FAITH

Now faith is confidence in what we hope for and assurance about what we do not see.

Hebrews 11:1 (NIV)

Faith is having complete trust, confidence, assurance, a firm conviction and a strong belief in God. Faith is confidence in what we hope for and the assurance that God is working, even though we cannot see it. Faith knows that no matter what the situation looks like, God is working on our behalf. Faith focuses on God and not the circumstances.

Humans make thousands of decisions every day. As we make these decisions, we need to remember to seek guidance and direction. When we walk it out in faith, we are:

> **F**acing
> **A**ll
> **I**ndecisions
> **T**hrough
> **H**im

As we encounter obstacles or adversity in life, we have to make decisions. In those moments of indecision, we need to decide to walk in faith. When we are consumed with the situation, our vision can become clouded, like we have cataracts. When we shift our focus to faith, the cataracts are removed and we can clearly see the path God has set before us. The path that God shows us through faith may look different than what was expected. We cannot let any naysayers try to discourage us and make us play small when God has instructed us on how to handle a situation.

Remember that God is always faithful. We may waver, but God is always steadfast and immovable. Have faith in God, He has never lost a battle!

'F.A.I.T.H.'

Day 23

VICTORY

The Lord your God wins victory after victory and is always with you. He celebrates and sings because of you and He will refresh your life with His love.

Zephaniah 3:17 (CEV)

*T*o have victory means to overcome an enemy; to achieve mastery or success in a struggle or endeavor against odds or difficulties; winning in a competition over an opponent or difficult problems.

How many of you remember the high school cheerleaders leading the crowd with V-I-C-T-O-R-Y? As they chanted each letter, the crowd would scream back with the letter and at the end they would ask what does that spell? Everyone would shout VICTORY!!! As we think back on those days, we remember how exciting it was to have won the game and to be able to shout Victory!

Fast forward to adulthood. God wants us to be just excited when we have victories over satan and his shenanigans. Adult challenges can be a bit more daunting than a high school football game. However, we know that with God as the coach, victory is inevitable! Even though there may be feelings of hopelessness, despair, or like all is lost, God is saying the game is not over if you trust me. He loves us with a never ending love. A love that energizes and empowers us to run on to the end, so we can see the VICTORY!

'We Win!'

Day 24

ACCOUNTABILITY

Therefore, each one must answer for himself and give a personal account of his own life before God.

Romans 14:12 (TPT)

One definition of accountability implies a willingness to be judged on performance. Accountability is also an acceptance of responsibility for honest and ethical conduct. Transparency, which involves collecting information and making it available and accessible for public scrutiny is a component of accountability.

How many of you have ever joined a challenge where you had to post your daily results on social media? There are tons of challenges out there. Some challenges are free, however some come with a price. Well, let me be transparent and go ahead and raise my hand for both. I would always say I would actually walk more steps, drink more water, or do more of whatever the challenge entailed, if I had to post it where someone else would see my results. God showed me that I was really just trying to look good in front of other people. I was more concerned about what people in the challenge thought about how I was crushing the challenge.

God asked me why did I need to be accountable to someone else for *my health*? My physical and spiritual well-being should be important enough to me to want to do what is necessary for me without paying to show someone else I am reaching my goals. God also told me that He is my accountability partner and that I can partner with Him for free! God's grace is sufficient!

'Partner With God'

Day 25

CLUTTER/ DECLUTTER

But all things must be done appropriately and in an orderly manner.

I Corinthians 14:40 (AMP)

*C*lutter is to fill or cover with scattered or disordered things that impede movement or reduce effectiveness.

Declutter is to remove mess or clutter from a place; to organize, prioritize, simplify and get rid of disorder.

Clutter can be physical as well as mental. Let's look at clutter as it relates to your mind and your thoughts. How many of you are not moving forward because you keep looking back? Your mind is cluttered with the guilt of your past. Your mind is cluttered with the many times you have failed over and over. Your thoughts are cluttered with what people think about you. Your thoughts are cluttered with all your self imposed limitations.

It is time to **DECLUTTER!** In addition to clearing out your mind and thoughts, you also need to declutter your environment. What do your closets look like? Are you able to eat at your kitchen table or is it covered with mail? Are you able to sit at your desk and work or do you have to clear out a spot for your computer? You may not realize it, but living in situations like the ones described can lead to chaos and confusion in your mind. If your surroundings are neat and organized, it decreases your stress level and allows you to be more productive. It allows you to be able to sit quietly with God and sort things out in your mind. It allows you to realize that God's Word is true and you can stand on I Corinthians 2:16b that states you have the mind of Christ. It will allow you to silence the noise and clearly hear from God as you stand in your power!

'Mind Freedom'

Day 26

ELOHE CHASEDDI GOD OF MERCY

Let us have confidence then and approach God's throne, where there is grace. There we will receive mercy and find grace to help us just when we need it.

Hebrews 4:16 (GNT)

Mercy is defined as compassion, kindly forbearance or forgiveness shown toward someone whom it is within one's power to punish or harm. God shows His mercy for those who are suffering through healing, comfort, the alleviation of suffering and caring about those in distress. His mercy shows up in the believer's life at salvation and continues to show mercy in forgiveness.

Mercy in Hebrew

- Racham means to love or have compassion
- Kapporeth means ransom and it is associated with the mercy seat
- Chesed means goodness, kindness or mercifulness

God's mercy gives us a second chance. Elohe Chaseddi, God of mercy showers us with forgiveness and bathes us with lovingkindness. Even when we make mistakes, if we love Him and ask for His forgiveness, God is forever willing to offer forgiveness to a repentant heart. He is always compassionate. We always have access to the peace of mind that God so freely gives in abundance. He promises to be with us always and bring us through every situation.

'God's Mercy'

Day 27

FORGIVE

Lay aside bitter words, temper tantrums, revenge, profanity and insults. But instead be kind and affectionate toward one another. Has God graciously forgiven you? Then graciously forgive one another in the depth of Christ's love.

Ephesians 4:31-32 (TPT)

When you forgive someone, you should stop feeling angry or resentful for an offense, flaw or mistake. This is often easier said than done. First of all, you must admit how angry you are and who is the cause of the anger. Secondly, you must make a conscious decision to forgive the other person. Holding in anger can produce stress chemicals that can cause physical, mental and emotional sickness. It can also block God's ability to carry out His purpose and plan for your life.

Forgiveness is more for the person who was wronged. In order to move forward in life and walk in peace, forgiveness is a must. When you refuse to forgive, you give your power away. It is truly not worth it to fall into Satan's trap and walk around powerless when you have dominion and authority! Make today the day that you take back your power and walk in forgiveness!

'Let It Go'

GRATITUDE

Let everyone give all their praise and thanks to the Lord! Here's why–He's better than anyone could ever imagine. Yes, He's always loving and kind and His faithful love never ends.

Psalm 107:1 (TPT)

*G*ratitude is the quality of being thankful; readiness to show appreciation for and to return kindness. A person who feels gratitude is thankful for what he has and focuses on the blessings received. He realizes God is sufficient and does not dwell or complain about what he doesn't have. Gratitude is an important part of worship. It honors and glorifies God when we show Him the gratitude He deserves.

Let's look at a couple of ways to cultivate a Spirit of Gratitude. Counting your blessings is a great way. We often take our everyday blessings for granted. Blessings such as a comfortable bed, clean running water and lights at the flip of a switch. These things are second nature to us, but we must remember to be grateful for them. A second way is to be intentional by putting thoughts into words. This can be as simple as making a list of what you are grateful for or keeping a gratitude journal. Let's start and end each day with an attitude of gratitude!

'Be Thankful'

Day 29

FAVOR

For the Lord God is brighter than the brilliance of a sunrise! Wrapping Himself around me like a shield, He is so generous with his gifts of grace and glory. Those who walk along His paths with integrity will never lack one thing they need, for He provides it all.

Psalms 84:11 (TPT)

*F*avor is receiving an act of kindness beyond what is due or usual; receiving approval or preference over others; having something done or granted out of goodwill, rather than from justice or earnings. Favor is also exhibited by others when they use their influence, power and resources on our behalf.

Scripture tells us in Psalms 5:12 that the Lord will bless the righteous and His favor will surround them like a shield. How awesome it is to have God's favor going before you to prepare the way. The favor of God will cause people to go out of their way to bless you without even knowing why they are doing it. God's supernatural favor flowing in your life is not based on pedigree, looks or personality. God's favor is based on the Word of God and believing what it says about you. Believing that you are highly favored by God will cause you to experience great victories, supernatural turnarounds and miraculous breakthroughs in the midst of great impossibilities! God's favor supersedes natural circumstances.

'I have Uncommon Favor'

Day 30

INTEGRITY

If you are good, you are guided by honesty. People who can't be trusted are destroyed by their own dishonesty.

Proverbs 11:3 (GNT)

*I*ntegrity is the quality of being honest and having strong moral principles. It is being complete, unbroken or unimpaired. Integrity is an unwavering determination of the heart to do right no matter what. A person of integrity will do right even when no one is watching. The person of integrity will not unload the groceries and leave the shopping cart in the middle of the parking space. You may think, what's the big deal? It's just a shopping cart! What in the world does that have to do with being honest? Another part of that definition is strong moral principles. These are guidelines people live by to make sure they are doing the right thing. It is doing the right thing to place the shopping cart in the appropriate place when you are finished.

Let's talk about another great example of walking in integrity. How many non-handicapped people park in handicap parking spaces? It is understood that there are many legitimate reasons why a person may have a handicap decal. Sometimes these reasons may not be something that can be physically seen by others, so do not be quick to assume that they are parking illegally. However, there are those multitudes of people who park in the spaces out of convenience.

If you are one of those parking in a handicap space out of convenience, think about the person who has a walker or the person in a wheelchair who isn't able to walk from the back of the parking lot. Maybe you said it won't matter, I'll just be a few minutes. Maybe you thought no one saw you when you parked. Remember that God sits high, looks low and keeps good books. Selah! As you go through your day, think about your actions and make sure you are doing the right thing even when you think no one is looking.

'God Sees You'

ABOUT THE AUTHOR

Sandra is a multifaceted individual. She is a wife and mother, healthcare worker, author and parallel-preneur. Sandra is a "people" person. She has a heart for people and wants to see others win in life. She often gives all praise to God for the wins in her life.

This Be Still devotional is a reminder to us that the way to the winner's circle is through partnering with God! He wants to see His children win in life. When God is involved, all you do is win, win, win no matter what!

Sandra lives in Pleasant Grove, AL with her husband Harrell. They have three sons, Mychal, Tevyn and Trynton.